HELLO!

This book was inspired by the amazing teens in my life who didn't quite realise just how great they were. I hope it'll inspire you to discover the best version of yourself and tackle challenges that come your way.

If you found this book useful, I'd love to hear from you. Send me a note at iona@30everafter.com with the subject line: I've got this.

ABOUT ME

Time I Wake Up

Usual Breakfast

Most Played Song

Last TV Show Watched

Favorite Book

Current Food Craving

My Safe Space

Your values make up who you are

What are some things you value?
What are your beliefs?

MY PERSONAL MANIFESTO

An essay about myself.

What are my core values and beliefs?

What am I doing right now to honor them?

What other things can I do to reinforce them?

Life is not
a dress rehearsal

Defining your purpose

How matters most to you?

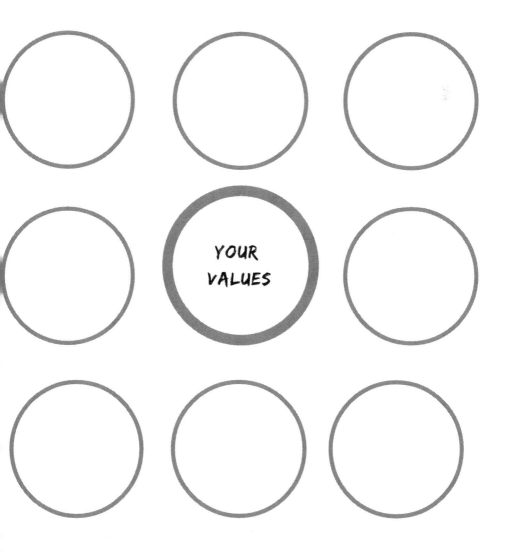

YOUR VALUES

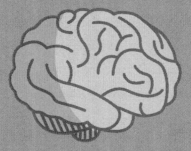

TRAINING YOUR BRAIN

DID YOU KNOW...?

If you want to be successful in anything you do, the best place to start is by training your brain. The most successful people use a growth mindset approach to help them tackle any challenge!

GROWTH MINDSET

VERSUS

FIXED MINDSET

"I'm not good at most school subjects".

"I can learn anything I want".

"I failed that test".

"I have a second opportunity to learn".

"This is going to be too difficult for me".

"Nothing is too difficult for me".

HAPPINESS ISN'T ABOUT THE DESTINATION.

It's about the journey.

-Unknown

RECIPE TO HAPPINESS

Learn what makes you happy

Think about the moments that make you happy.
Who was there? What were you doing?
Write down your recipe for happiness.

For every minute you are angry, you lose 60 seconds of happiness.

- Ralph Waldo Emerson

KEEPING CALM

Coping Strategies

There are many things that cause stress in our daily lives. What are some things you can do to cope with stress?

BODY IMAGE

Coping Strategies

Don't let a scale measure your self worth.

BODY IMAGE

Coping Strategies

The 'perfect' body isn't always the one you see on Instagram. Sometimes the images we see online are manipulated through photo editing tools.

What does the perfect body look like to you? Sketch it out here.

BODY IMAGE Q&A

Use the following writing prompts as a body image check-in.

I feel the best about my body when...

I'm in my best shape when...

To me a perfect body is a...

BODY IMAGE Q&A

Use the following writing prompts as a body image check-in.

What I can do to stay in shape...

The people who inspire me to be healthy are...

When it comes to my body, my goal is to...

I FEEL AWESOME ABOUT MYSELF WHEN...

EVERYONE SEES SUCCESS DIFFERENTLY. WHAT MAKES YOU FEEL AWESOME? IS IT GETTING AN 'A' ON A REPORT? FEELING FIT AND HEALTHY? JOT THEM DOWN HERE.

I FEEL AWESOME ABOUT MYSELF WHEN...

EVERYONE SEES SUCCESS DIFFERENTLY. WHAT MAKES YOU FEEL AWESOME? IS IT GETTING AN 'A' ON A REPORT? FEELING FIT AND HEALTHY? JOT THEM DOWN HERE.

BE YOUR OWN KIND OF AWESOME

- UNKNOWN

MIRROR, MIRROR

WHO DO YOU SEE
WHEN YOU LOOK IN THE MIRROR?

Think of six words to describe what you see in the mirror.

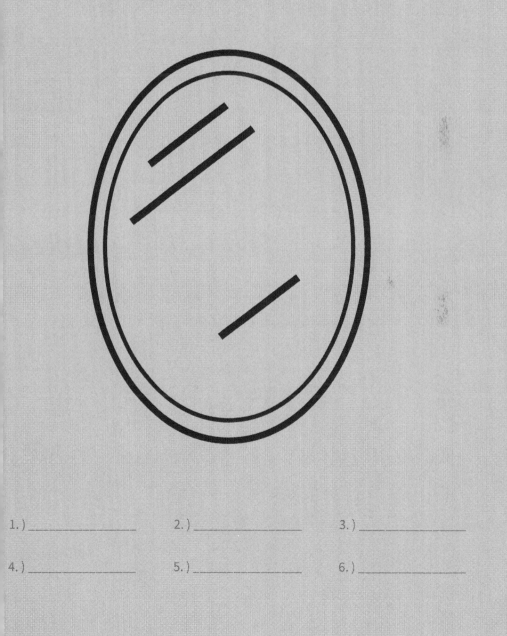

1.) _____   2.) _____   3.) _____

4.) _____   5.) _____   6.) _____

my feelings in emojis

CURRENT MOOD:

EMOJI I USE A LOT:

FAVORITE ANIMAL:

EMOJI THAT LOOKS LIKE ME:

FAVORITE DRINK:

HOW MY FAMILY SEES ME

INTERVIEW A FAMILY MEMBER

INTERVIEWEE   DATE

WHAT ARE THREE WORDS YOU'D USE TO DESCRIBE ME?

WHAT ARE MY STRENGTHS?

WHAT IS SOMETHING I'M REALLY GOOD AT?

WHAT IS YOUR FAVOURITE MEMORY OF US?

HOW MY FAMILY SEES ME

INTERVIEW A FAMILY MEMBER

INTERVIEWEE   DATE

WHAT ARE THREE WORDS YOU'D USE TO DESCRIBE ME?

WHAT ARE MY STRENGTHS?

WHAT IS SOMETHING I'M REALLY GOOD AT?

WHAT IS YOUR FAVOURITE MEMORY OF US?

HOW MY FRIEND SEES ME

INTERVIEW A FRIEND

INTERVIEWEE   DATE

WHAT ARE THREE WORDS YOU'D USE TO DESCRIBE ME?

WHAT ARE MY STRENGTHS?

WHAT IS SOMETHING I'M REALLY GOOD AT?

WHAT IS YOUR FAVOURITE MEMORY OF US?

HOW MY FRIEND SEES ME

INTERVIEW A FRIEND

INTERVIEWEE   DATE

WHAT ARE THREE WORDS YOU'D USE TO DESCRIBE ME?

WHAT ARE MY STRENGTHS?

WHAT IS SOMETHING I'M REALLY GOOD AT?

WHAT IS YOUR FAVOURITE MEMORY OF US?

ONLINE BULLIES

What people say about you says alot more about them than you.
-Unknown

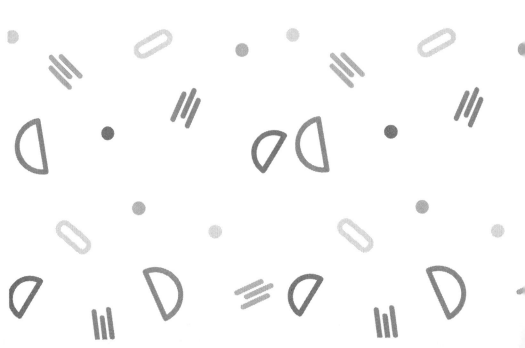

ONLINE BULLIES

HAVE YOU EVER ENCOUNTERED CYBER BULLYING?

HOW DID YOU DEAL?

The last time I experienced cyber bullying was...

It made me feel...

I dealt with it by...

If my friends are being bullied online or in person, I will...

Use your imagination

Write a story based on your favorite TV show.

Use your imagination

Continue your story...

AFFIRMATIONS

YOUR WORDS.
YOUR REALITY.

We all have bad days but if we are armed with the right tools, bad days won't last long. Affirmations can help shift your mindset so you can see each situation as an opportunity. Come up with your own list of affirmations.

AFFIRMATION TO USE WHEN I'M FRUSTRATED:

AFFIRMATION TO USE WHEN I'M LONLEY:

AFFIRMATION TO USE WHEN I'M SAD:

YOUR WORDS.
YOUR REALITY.

AFFIRMATIONS

AFFIRMATION TO USE WHEN I DON'T FEEL
GREAT ABOUT MYSELF:

AFFIRMATION TO USE WHEN I MAKE A
MISTAKE:

AFFIRMATION TO USE WHEN I DON'T
UNDERSTAND SOMETHING:

AFFIRMATION TO USE WHEN I RECEIVE TEST
RESULTS I DID NOT EXPECT:

WORRYING IS LIKE PAYING A DEBT YOU DON'T OWE.

- MARK TWAIN

THE WORRY JAR

LIFE GETS BUSY AND CHAOTIC REGARDLESS OF YOUR AGE.
SOMETIMES IT'S EASIER TO RELEASE YOUR WORRIES FROM YOUR
MIND BY WRITING IT DOWN.

MY DREAM SUMMER VACATION

IF YOU COULD PLAN YOUR SUMMER VACATION, WHAT WOU
IT LOOK LIKE? WHO WOULD YOU BRING? WHERE WOULD YO
GO?

MY DREAM SUMMER VACATION

_____

_____

_____

_____

_____

_____

_____

_____

_____

_____

_____

_____

_____

_____

WHAT DO YOU KNOW ABOUT LOVE?

THE PERFECT LOVE STORY

Love is a topic that's typically reserved for girls but it's a universal topic. Let's write out your perfect relationship. Stuck for ideas? Here are a few questions to get you started.

DO YOU BELIEVE IN LOVE AT FIRST SIGHT?

WHAT DOES LOVE LOOK AND FEEL LIKE TO YOU?

HAVE YOU EXPERIENCED LOVE BEFORE?

YOUR IDEAL RELATIONSHIP

WHAT DOES YOUR IDEAL RELATIONSHIP LOOK LIKE?

WHAT ARE QUALITIES OF A GOOD GUY?

WHAT DOES A HEALTHY RELATIONSHIP FEEL LIKE?

WHAT DOES YOUR IDEAL GUY LOOK LIKE?

HOW WOULD YOUR IDEAL GUY TREAT YOU?

DESCRIBE YOUR DREAM DATE

LOVE ROLE MODELS

There are many factors that can influence the way we love. Let's start by looking at examples of love you witness everyday.

Who are your love role models?

What do you admire about their relationships?

What have you learned from their relationships?

How can you use the relationships you admire to improve your reationships?

LUCK IS SOMETHING YOU CREATE

WHAT WOULD YOU DO WITH ONE MILLION DOLLARS?

MY BUCKET LIST

AN ESSAY ABOUT THE THINGS I WANT TO DO.

Share ten things you'd like to try before you reach a certain age.

MY BUCKET LIST

AN ESSAY ABOUT THE THINGS I WANT TO DO.

Share ten things you'd like to try before you reach a certain age.

"LIFE IS EITHER A DARING ADVENTURE OR NOTHING"

- HELEN KELLER

PLACES TO GO

If you can dream it, you can do it.

Directions: Mark off a few places you'd like to travel to.

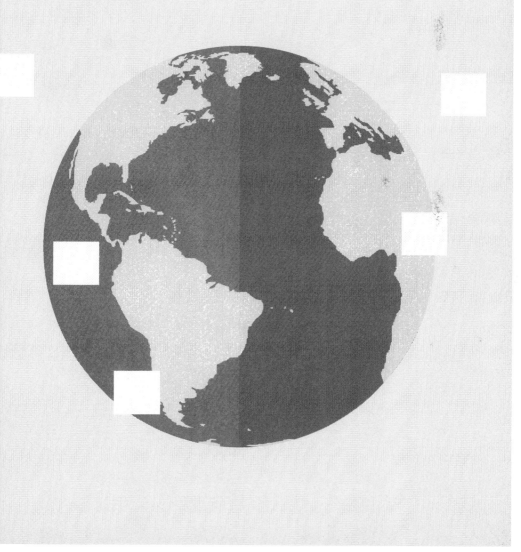

My Top 10

WHAT ARE TOP 10 THINGS YOU'D LIKE TO
DO/HAVE/SEE THIS YEAR?

My Top 10

Understanding Your Emotions

There's no doubt that our emotions can get the best of us.The more we can articulate them, the better we can manage them. Take a few minutes to understand your range of emotions.

An emotion I experience often:	What it feels like:	What it looks like:

Understanding Your Emotions

There's no doubt that our emotions can get the best of us.The more we can articulate them, the better we can manage them. Take a few minutes to understand your range of emotions.

An emotion I experience often:	What it feels like:	What it looks like:

OVERNIGHT SUCCESS STORIES TAKE A LONG TIME.

- STEVE JOBS

STAR POWER

Despite what we see online, success doesn't happen over night. Even 'stars' you see online have put in hours, days and years to hone their craft. What do you want to be known for?

WHAT DO YOU WANT TO BE KNOWN FOR?

WHAT WILL YOU NEED TO LEARN/DO TO MAKE IT HAPPEN?

PRACTICING GRATITUDE

THERE ARE SO MANY THINGS TO BE THANKFUL FOR AND YET IT'S SO EASY TO LOSE SIGHT OF ALL THE LOVE AND THINGS WE HAVE AROUND US.

PRACTISING JUST THREE MINUTES OF GRATITUDE A DAY CAN CHANGE YOUR PERSPECTIVE ON LIFE.

TRY IT! EACH DAY WRITE THREE THINGS YOU'RE GRATEFUL FOR.

All the things I'm grateful for - Thank You

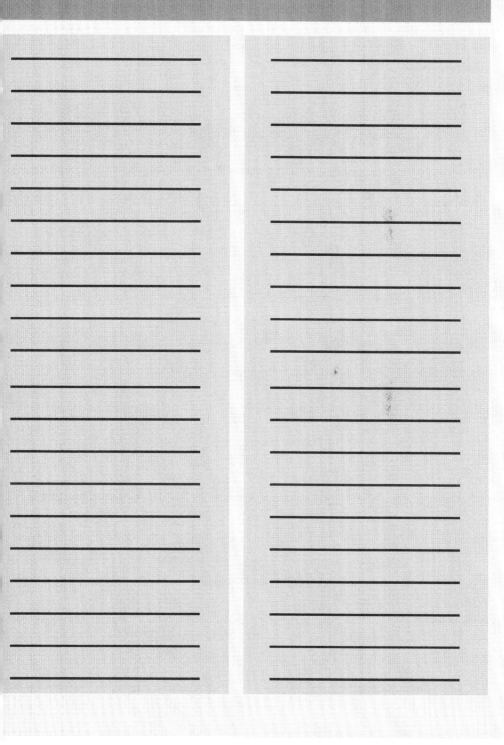

PRACTICING GRATITUDE

Journal Writing Exercise

Thinking about being thankful

Writing a journal helps you recognize your own feelings over certain things or events, no matter how mundane. For this exercise, use the following pages and write down at least 25 things that made you feel good today.

"Our life is shaped by our minds, for we become what we think"

- Buddha

A Personal Quiet Space

**EVERYONE COULD USE A PERSONAL SANCTUARY
- A HAPPY PLACE OF THEIR OWN.**

Map out your ideal quiet space.

STRESS BUSTERS

STRESSED? NO WORRIES.

If you have the tools to manage your stress, you'll be able to tackle any challenge that comes your way. Think of a list of things you can do when you feel stressed.

STRESS BUSTERS

STRESSED? NO WORRIES.

f you have the tools to manage your stress, you'll be able to tackle any challenge
hat comes your way. Think of a list of things you can do when you feel stressed.

UNPLUGGING

WHEN WE'RE CONSTANTLY CONNECTED TO OUR DEVICES IT'S
BEST TO TAKE SOME TIME OUT TO DISCONNECT. THINK ABOUT A
FEW THINGS YOU CAN DO TO RESET YOUR MIND.

UNPLUGGING

WHEN WE'RE CONSTANTLY CONNECTED TO OUR DEVICES IT'S BEST TO TAKE SOME TIME OUT TO DISCONNECT. THINK ABOUT A FEW THINGS YOU CAN DO TO RESET YOUR MIND.

"Fears are nothing but a state of mind"

Napolean Hill

WHAT AM I SCARED OF?

EVERYONE IS AFRAID OF SOMETHING

It's not always easy confronting your biggest fear?
Is it loneliness or failing an exam? Or is it a fear of
rejection? Write it down and share it with someone.

_____

_____

_____

_____

_____

_____

_____

_____

_____

_____

_____

_____

_____

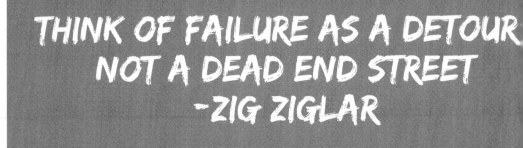

THINK OF FAILURE AS A DETOUR
NOT A DEAD END STREET
-ZIG ZIGLAR

EMBRACE YOUR FEARS

Everyone fails at some point but it's how you deal with failure that matters. Think about the challenges you've had and the lessons you've learned from them.

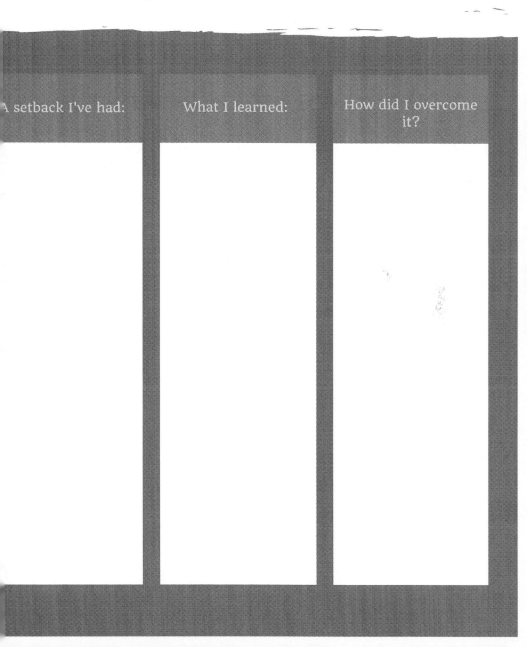

A setback I've had:	What I learned:	How did I overcome it?

KICKING GOALS

YOU CAN ACHIEVE ANYTHING
YOU SET YOUR MIND TO. FILL
OUT YOUR GOALS HERE AND
DON'T HOLD BACK.

GOAL 1:

GOAL 2

GOAL 3

GOAL 4

GOAL 5

KICKING GOALS

YOU CAN ACHIEVE ANYTHING
YOU SET YOUR MIND TO. FILL
OUT YOUR GOALS HERE AND
DON'T HOLD BACK.

GOAL 6:

GOAL 7:

GOAL 8:

GOAL 9:

GOAL 10:

LEARN SOMETHING NEW

The fastest way to grow is to learn something new. Take a new class and note what you've learned.

WHAT I KNOW:

_____
_____
_____
_____
_____

WHAT I WANT TO KNOW:

_____
_____
_____
_____
_____

WHAT I LEARNED:

_____
_____
_____
_____
_____

LEARN SOMETHING NEW

The fastest way to grow is to learn something new. Take a new class and note what you've learned.

WHAT I KNOW:

_____
_____
_____
_____
_____

WHAT I WANT TO KNOW:

_____
_____
_____
_____

WHAT I LEARNED:

_____
_____
_____
_____

MY SUPERHEROS

Who is someone you admire?
Write a list of all the things you admire about
him/her.

MY SUPERHEROS

Who is someone you admire?
Write a list of all the things you admire about
him/her.

"CHANGE YOUR MINDSET AND YOU'LL CHANGE YOUR WORLD"
- UNKNOWN

DAILY CHECK-IN

Take time to reflect on your day. Try it for 7 days and see what happens.

Date:

What did I learn today?

What is something I'm grateful for?

My biggest achievement of today was...

Something that inspired me was...

An act of kindness I witnessed was...

DAILY CHECK-IN

Take time to reflect on your day. Try it for 7 days and
see what happens.

Date:

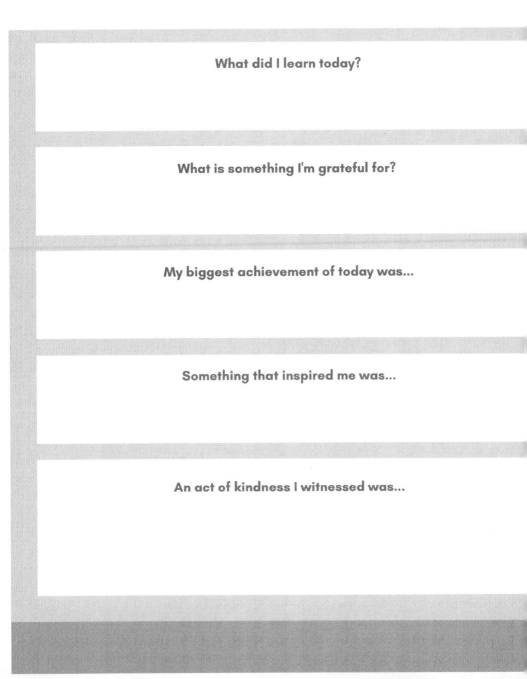

What did I learn today?

What is something I'm grateful for?

My biggest achievement of today was...

Something that inspired me was...

An act of kindness I witnessed was...

DAILY CHECK-IN

Take time to reflect on your day. Try it for 7 days and see what happens.

Date:

What did I learn today?

What is something I'm grateful for?

My biggest achievement of today was...

Something that inspired me was...

An act of kindness I witnessed was...

DAILY CHECK-IN

Take time to reflect on your day. Try it for 7 days and see what happens.

Date:

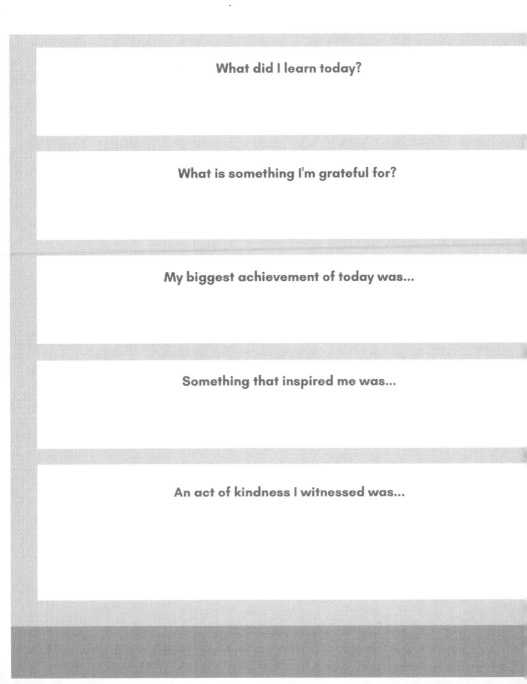

What did I learn today?

What is something I'm grateful for?

My biggest achievement of today was...

Something that inspired me was...

An act of kindness I witnessed was...

DAILY CHECK-IN

Take time to reflect on your day. Try it for 7 days and
see what happens.

Date:

What did I learn today?

What is something I'm grateful for?

My biggest achievement of today was...

Something that inspired me was...

An act of kindness I witnessed was...

DAILY CHECK-IN

Take time to reflect on your day. Try it for 7 days and see what happens.

Date:

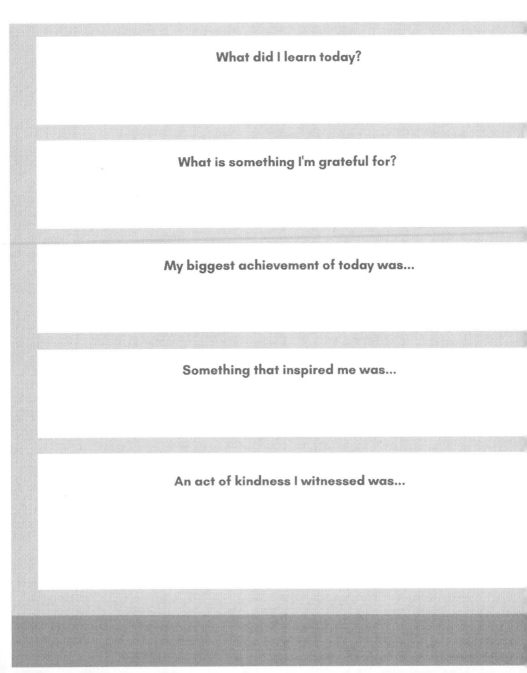

What did I learn today?

What is something I'm grateful for?

My biggest achievement of today was...

Something that inspired me was...

An act of kindness I witnessed was...

DAILY CHECK-IN

Take time to reflect on your day. Try it for 7 days and
see what happens.

Date:

What did I learn today?

What is something I'm grateful for?

My biggest achievement of today was...

Something that inspired me was...

An act of kindness I witnessed was...

FOR DOODLES & MUSINGS

FOR DOODLES & MUSINGS

FOR DOODLES & MUSINGS

FOR DOODLES & MUSINGS

FOR DOODLES & MUSINGS

FOR DOODLES & MUSINGS

66

You are
capable of
more than
you know

WHAT DID YOU THINK?

If you've reached this page I hope that you've realised how wonderful you truly are. If you enjoyed these pages, you might like other books.

OTHER BOOKS YOU MIGHT LIKE

QUESTIONS?

I love questions and feedback! Send me a note at
iona@30everafter.com.

Made in United States
Orlando, FL
16 September 2022

22497496R00057